A WORD FROM A PROPHET

PLUS

A PRACTICAL GUIDE TO REPENTENCE

Introduction

My true appeal. I am appealing to the Highest Court and to the Righteous Judge, God Almighty, YHWH. My plea is not only for myself but for the world to come into the Righteousness of the Almighty and do good, for the good of the whole. I am Prophet Meeko Carraway Inmate, diagnosed from birth with oxygen deprivation, then several mental illnesses, self-mutations, and self-medicating. Perhaps I am called into this Kingdom for such a time as this. See me, see my fate and that of millions. Intercessors must now intercede. The Most High will ask us to give an account for what we did, knowing the truth of the propaganda and exploitation of many of His children. All souls are His. This book is summary of my life in hopes that others will also see their need to repent, pray, intercede, and intervene early on behalf of the challenged and feeble minded.

Prior to the Regan administration, there were honest and effective efforts made to treat the mentally ill with therapy, counseling, diets, training, support and redirection. Patton State Hospital was once a prime example of positive interventions that worked. The Christian Community tried to introduce a better way of living. They did a lot of praying and talking but did not have the facilities to follow through. The Muslims did the greater work with the prison population in the 70s and 80s. Theirs was a better approach. They were able to retrain thousands to sell bean pies, newspapers and learn a healthier, more productive, and honorable way of living. They were able to slow the revolving doors to prisons and institutions down for a while.

Prescribed drugs and illegal drugs overtook progress. Drugs have become Slave Masters. Drugs sorcery causes one to feel better about bad conditions while making bad matters worst. It is also big business for both illegal and illegal drug pushers of America. Greed and deprivation promote mental illness, criminal activities and social misfunctioning. We cannot

pretend that we can not do any better. Many will answer for

the manipulation of deprived populations, The Most High,

Creator of the universe Is sitting high and looking low into the

events of mankind. Let the Record show that Prophet Meeko

Carraway has taken our cases to the Highest Court. I appeal to

Almighty God, the true Lawmaker and only Righteous Judge, in

the Name of Jesus the Christ, Yahshua Ha Mashiach and all that

is Holy. May His Mercy, Grace and Compassion overrule the

world of hidden misconduct. Have mercy on our souls.

ISRAEL TO YOU LORD

To You Lord I pray for my clean date June 5th 2020 to mean

something to me as I know that you want me sober and I want

to be I need your help with follow through because when I am

tested and enticed by my own lust I shall need your help to

stand firm. I am changing to the way of shunning the very

appearance of evil, not for profit or gain in this world but for

eternal life, An eternal priesthood where I may serve You day

and night I thank You for listening in responding, Amen.

Dear Father in heaven I pray Your strength comes over me and

make me strong enough to stay sober and glorify your Name I

pray Your Spirit will dwell in in me in a real way and not without

all power to save me from my desires to be altered. I want to

witness that there is no God but You, no mighty one whom You

do not know You are great and mighty. I will serve You in this

way I will respect my clean date my second or third birthday. I

will preach without hypocrisy Amen

Dear Lord, You know my struggles in all it entails I pray that You give me the savvy to do it right without revealing what's going on in the inmate world I thank you for bringing me to a place that I don't want a substance in my body and that just for today I will fight the good fight for sobriety. Be my God and Father so that you open Your hand and release to me Power over my lust. The lust of the eye, the flesh and heart. Send angelic workers Father to bill and plant in me all that I need for this endeavor Amen

Dear Lord I love your discipline an reproved handle me with care be careful my Lord with my chest arising so that you do not break my mind and heart my hope is continuously of you be strong for me and do not relent fix my troubles in my mind and heart hope for the best I hope for the best and care for the worse be a shelter for me to live in always from my troubles I fear the end the light in though those that do the same be strong for me and shelter me in all my ways that may never be overwhelmed by my enemies I am always thankful of you Amen.

Dear Lord I pray for the pressure upon my soul to be eased so that I can relax. I truly want to represent Your strength to the world so that Your Power can be seen by all that see me overcome by prayer and submission to you. I can be seen by many as a person who overcame by the Power of God, Even I can only overcome by the Power of You my Lord Take me by the hand Lord and lead me along the path of life so that I can glorify You in all that I do in Jesus Name Amen.

Dear Lord I pray for strength in this isolation that I will weather this storm like a champion with ease. I hope for a strong hand from the Lord in all the trouble. I hoped to see a strong hand from You to help me in my time of need. I do not know what else to ask for just help me through this hard time. I hope You will be moved to help because I know You can. You are great and mighty able to save from every sort of affliction. I thank

You for Your help and in Jesus Name I love You for Your help

Amen

Dear Lord help me with my time management I pray for better outlooks on time and better results from thinking about time. People have harder time than me to put up with. Not that this should be the best for my prayers I just want to feel better about my situation. I hope that You will see what is going on and fix some of the discomfort mental mentalities that come from the isolation discomfort. I pray for the people that want to kill me. I pray for peace with them in every way possible. I hope for Your help Lord in every way in Jesus name Amen. Praise Yahshua Ha Mashiach.

Dear Lord I have sufficient amount of coffee operated I will use it wisely and drink it appropriately I must maintain my sleep and awake cycle and not stress in isolation. I also must stay active in isolation but not overdo it and ruin a good thing. This will require restraints at appropriate times I pray that this incentives drive is salted by your Spirit and Truth. I can hope now that it is to You and I have recorded my prayers. I know you will respond, help me pass the long hours with TV and sleep in silence not with the music on thank you Lord Amen, in Yahshua's Name Amen

Dear Lord, I go to my cross as Yahshua went to His cross. I accept that I must go like my Master when I thank you for the mindset an opportunity to lay down my life for Jesus the best friend I ever had. I pray that when penitentiary poverty comes upon me, I'll stand with arms wide and heart abandoned in awe of the One who gave His all. He encouraged us to do the same. I gladly go to my death uncertain as it is. To die like a sheep so I can be raised in God's Power forever more Amen. In Jesus' Name.

Dear Lord, I am grateful for the way I have overcome fear of death being gathered to Christ all I want out of this life is death unto heaven. This is the goal of this existence since the fall of man. I am not afraid of being stabbed to death for my sins against mankind I'll standfast till you let the evil one overcome me and kill me like Christ was killed. Paul was killed, all the apostles were killed, and all the believers must take up their cross in righteousness and go to the place of the skull. Death where is your sting in Yahshua's Name. Thank you. Amen.

Dear Lord, I pray that I can present my body daily as a living sacrifice, fasting from lunch daily. I will eat solid food only twice a day, after breakfast is done. I will fast until dinner. Sir. help me base my life around this endeavor to remove a filthy and unclean spirits from me. Help me to clearly understand the Word of the Lord when I receive it. I pray for contentment to mark my behavior and that I will be found waiting on the Lord when death finds me in Jesus Name Amen.

Dear Lord, I view death a new beginning where I will be gathered to my people. Believers who have died all manners of death before me. I fear not the piercing of my flesh or the suffocating of my lungs. Death is not my end but my rebirth into the Kingdom of God. I, as an heir, I love your Commands and vowed to love it all my days and time around wicked or upright men. With your help I am able to keep Your Love in all

circumstances, looking forward to being gathered unto Christ

and the day of my death. Amen in Jesus Name Amen

Dear You Lord, I am grateful for the way I have overcome fear of

death being gathered to Christ. All I want out of this life is to

enter heaven. This is the goal of this existence since the fall of

man. I am not afraid of being stabbed to death for my sins

against mankind. Help me to be standfast till you let the evil

one overcome me and kill me like Christ was killed. Paul was

killed all the apostles were killed. All believers must take up

their cross in righteousness and go to the place of the skull.

Death where is your sting? In Yahshua's Name, thank You Amen

Dear Lord I cannot fast even from lunch by choice so I will try to

keep Your Commands and live life loving people. Can you please

forgive me because I cannot fast? I hope that in the future I will

master my body and fast more. I need to be more disciplined,

but I cannot manage time or actions as I would like to. I must

select certain options and do them. I am not giving up

completely, I am just going down the safest path for now. Show me a better way if you will. I am sorry In Jesus Name Amen

Dear Lord, I'm grateful in isolation because of all the things You allowed me to process. I thank You for not letting me taste the property that I deserve for not putting in leg work like I was supposed to in order to support myself. I pray that you let me learn drawing so I can support myself in prison earning cosmetics and others stuff I need. I pray that I it will be able to apply myself and my time to this new path of art. I need your blessings in this and in all things, I do in Yahshua's Name. Amen.

Dear Lord, I pray for help and thriving in isolation. You have shown me that You can help me thrive in isolation. I thank you for hearing my prayers and also, answering me. I feel like I am empowered by You to take on the issue that come up with this form of isolation. I know that I can do all things through Your Spirit that strengthens me. Thank You for standing in the fire with me in my ongoing isolation. By Your Spirit I say I love isolation It is a valuable challenge to endure mentally. Thank You Lord for answering my prayer in Yahshua's name Amen

Dear Lord, now I believe prayers such as these are working because I see the difference in my life as I pray these prayers in a very hard time in my life. Your spirit makes changes for me to live with and to do better. I thank you for answering such a person as I am. I am not pure man but a great beast that has no ability to do for himself. I never have had the right ideas in time to save myself from discomfort. You do well at making sure I survived all my foolish choices, conscious or unconscious. Thank you for survival until now. It is a real miracle in Jesus Name

Dear Lord, this isolation is lingering and now food is shorter for us inmates. We only get a sack lunch for dinner. I know you can give me all the ability I need to handle this, but I feel the need to ask You for help me make the best of this here situation. Help me handle the cell time and the food shortage. I thank You that we get food at all. Do not think I'm not grateful I just want to be sure I have sufficient supplies for my needs. I thank

You for listening to me and I pray also You answer me. Your servant Israel in Jesus' Name Amen.

This is the book of the Prophet Israel yeah, Yahshay Shay Israel, I am here to declare Yahshua is Lord and is on his way back. He is coming as a lion to kill his prey who was set apart from the beginning of time. Time is about up for those in the Valley of Decision you must choose whom you will serve. We are about to be there. There is no double minded, two-way street. You must bow to Yahshua to gather with Him or refuse and be counted as being against Him. Our behavior is less important than who you choose to bow to. To whom you bow to is all important, so one must choose his words wisely. Who we bow to is indicated by our words. Even our profession of faith is first spoken in faith. Then we must try to get our actions in line with His Will. This, we cannot do alone, we need divine inner intervention to stop sinning.

 I was thrown by this realization, but it makes sense because the good I tried and swore to do I could not do, but the evil that I swore I would not do that I did. Therefore, I urge you to worry

more over what you say than what you do. What you do, God

will bring into obedience in due time if you continue strong in

your profession of faith. We cannot be perfect without the Spirit

of Yahweh enabling us to resist our own evil desires so that we

overcome ourselves in favor of the God we profess. Fear God

and resist bad company for the actions of mankind are contrary

to the Will of God. We must prophesy in the face of wicked

men and women folks. Our hope is the meat of Salvation. I urge

you to hope for the Spirit to save you from the world around

you because you cannot save yourself. Without God's help I

declare salvation on your own is your mirrors is false hope. As

the Lord judges men on a spectrum we all are found upon.

Where our actions can seem lacking to others so that we cannot

look down our nose at anyone in God's eyes. Any transgression

is a transgression against the Crown which is a call for death of

the sinner. Who can they pass condemnation on? Only the fool

passes condemnation upon themselves even I have to be

careful of what or who I judge for whatever reason. I decided not to judge any. I just n forgive all who have hurt me I will offer my life to those who wish to kill me. I will surrender my wealth to the Lord, no, I will not hold is dearly.

Murders. I have killed two people and as a Prophet I wonder why. Is a man one was evil another was God's will because I was under strong delusions when I killed the second person? I believe I was killing to create a sacred place to worship the Lord free from evil company, like my own little Promised land Like the children of Israel killed to obtain a place where they could worship YHWH and not have to deal with Pagan religions clouding their judgment by their presence in the Promised Land. I feel for the Israelites of old because when you go out there on faith and start a war on your faith in what YHWH is telling you, you are out there with no parachute. A world where the people are more in number than you, stronger than you and more able than you. All you have is your faith in YHWH. Naturally, it is uncomfortable. Those who held faith without failing in the Old Testament were truly Warriors of faith as you are trusting

YHWH to stop the mighty men of the war of the world from

murdering you, for obeying the Lord. They stood fast

undisturbed by the opposition, trusting in the visible defense of

an invisible God. The one I have come to put my trust in.

 I say that you will know me by my end and not by my

beginning. In my beginning I was born Second in the Judge

Carraway marriage. I was severely victimized as a young boy. I

was turned inside out by the circumstances of my young life.

This left me in a non-normal disposition I acted out by first

hurting family pets and graduated to people. I was like two

people one was nice and loving, the other was unsympathetic

an even unable to feel for the people he hurt for a time. Later,

the remorse would flood in like a wave of emotions creating a

cycle of love, pain, pressure, and remorse. I hurt and I have

hurt others. I tried to control my behavior but there was so

much cognitive dissonance that I could not settle down and

choose my destiny by mapping out my decisions. Decisions,

conscious or unconscious are yours to live with. I pray that I find forgiveness with the God of my Lord Yahshua Mashiach as I have sinned over and over again. I want to be righteous in my heart, but I am a sinner by my activities under the sun. This is why I tattooed the words, Blood of Jesus up on my chest plate. I need forgiveness and a holy cleansing so that the sins that so easily fall on my plate will not be consumed willingly. And thereby saving me from my evil desires that give rise to temptation and sin in my life.

Salvation. I am saved by grace through faith and in my life will show it in the end but God must increase in my conscious mind and stop letting my mind become overwhelmed by temptation so that I do things I wish I would not do and think. The things that I wish to do reside just outside my capability. Not saying I am not responsible for my actions but rather for me to reside in the Word and Wisdom of Yahweh. I need the supernatural strength of the Holy Spirit to manifest in my life, in my mind when I am troubled by the Valley of Decisions. Help me fight off my own desires to feel, see, do and act or say things. I will overcome evil desires and reign with Christ as the finisher of my faith

Faith is the evidence of things unseen. All that I do has a place in the Book of Faith. if I sin, I sin before the Father. If I sin not, I am saved by Grace of the Father. So, if I do good or evil God is present with me. I believe that Yah walks with us in darkness and in light. In darkness to understand and meditate, and in light to reward and exalt the righteous. So, He has no need of revelation into the past of anyone for He was there to see all that transpired. Faith is hope for God's activity in your life. I pray for His continuing activity in my life. I hope that my death would glorify the King of Glory as my life has been broken over and over. I pray that God may even be glorified in my brokenness so that I too may stan fast in my earthen vessel as a partaker of the glorious strength that is faith

Hope is what keeps me going, hope that I see and hear God working things out in my life for my good. I pray that all that happens to me works for all good. Be it hardship or pleasant things I care not about what I get in this life. My hope is for an eternal place of protection and happiness where I do not have to defend myself or be fearful that I may hurt someone else. God is always clear when we are hearing Him but when He hides His face, even though you called out to him this is when hope comes alive giving us the will to continue down the road. Certainty is given and taken by the Spirit. It is given in times of plenty and taken when times are tough. When we are in that pit we wonder if we heard God correctly are if perhaps, we were used or tricked. But. I urge you to hope in the Lord if you are or if you are wrong. The Lord reaps where He did not plant and exact things from His enemies so it may be that when your hope is set on Yahweh that He will reap your harvest because you set your hope on Him and you waiver not.

Will the Lord acquit the guilty? Never. But has not Christ paid the penalty for us all therefore forgiveness is for the guilty and faith is the hope of forgiveness. I am guilty of so many sins, yet I dwell in a pure heart. My hope set on the Father to cleanse my heart and purify my ways in the Word so that I too may walk completely upright before Him. in the face of the wicked and unrighteous in heart, I pray that my behavior meets His approval. Hearing the Lord, yes, I hear the Lord, but He is not at my disposal. Meaning I hear what He says to me, but I also talked to Him without getting a response. He does not jump when I say so. He does not give a Word for every heartache I have in the world. It is almost like I am meant to struggle for answers to people and their tribulations to have a Word to stand on. Not a word to give to people.

 Prophecies or the spirit of the prophets is simply the gift of faith in Yeshua and an urge to preach the truth of Yeshua in any situation or circumstances. I have preached in the drug houses, to witches and warlocks. I have preached high and sober. I have preached in faith and in doubt, but I have always prophesied about Yeshua and His Kingdom. I will continue to make His Way straight in the eyes of the Father and in the care of Yahshua, the only King of all things, past and present. The Ruler of all things whom Satan himself bows down to for fear of the torment. Better the time of the end of this present darkness which is spoken of. This darkness is because God uses darkness to hide the light from the minds of the loss so that they would not see Him except by diligently seeking Him by faith so that no one can say I need not a Savior. Nor can they say that they are righteous because of their own right hand.

 Right hand. I tattooed Servant of, Ahiah Ashar Ahiah, on my right hand so as to marry my hand of authority to the Most High. Therefore, all that are within my house as a man in this world would be in the authority of Yahweh by my marriage to Yahweh. I tattooed a wedding band on my right ring finger to signify my vow to give my authority to Yahweh for good or for or I believe Yahweh is God. I'm betting on him to save me now and later. I know that one day my God will come for me, to show up on my behalf and save me from my pain and suffering. Until then I will hope against hope that what I see and hear in the Spirit Is what it is. The guarantee that Yahweh is on my side and is also fixing me to be all that I was meant to be. To show

up means for Yahweh to move people in a way as for them to

approve of me an attribute my attribute my faith and hope in

God to a true faith and hope in Yahweh or show Himself to be

for me as my God in the eyes of the people. This is what

matters to me. I know not if God cares what people think of me

in my faith mostly because I am not privileged to that type of

information. My information is in God's presence and the fear

of God. I am sure that God will reveal the true nature of our

relationship to the people but in His own time, for His own

reasons. I prayed that I handled the road between here and

there well. I pray that I live well and that I die well before my

God who is my strength in whom I put all my trust. Looking at

my life I wonder why anyone would think I was a Prophet I

never done anything major and I've always had a drug habit

even though I was a preaching drug addict. I pray that my

behavior lines up with my prophesying of faith and I and that I

am not a hypocrite in the eyes of men. I understand that being

penetrated as a 6-year-old created some emotional baggage

that might attract addictive behavior. But time is up for children and childhood excuses for behavior. It is time to do better even though I live in a concentration of sinners, abusing drugs in my face I need the Lord to give me the will to stand and stay under the cover of faith and not yield to the will of the flesh. Although the Word does say give wine to him who has sorrow of heart it does not say be given to wine if you have sorrow of heart. So that it is the difference to use or to be used.

 Homosexuality, bisexual, I have been bisexual since 6 before I knew I was created a sexual identity as a man. I am heterosexual but I know butt stuff feels good so where does that leave me? I will tell you just playing with my butt on my own if at all. I had sex with a male in prison once and is not for me. No matter what people think. I am presently a gang associated which I am leaving mostly behind me as I cannot keep the command to love my enemies as a gang member no more than I can forgive and punish at the same time. I hope that I am killed for leaving the gang life for God. That is martyrdom which is a blessing in wolves clothing. I pray that I leave gang life and refuse to practice or participate and lose my life because of it, or I get killed for killing my cellie, that too is martyrdom. I was killing in the name of Yahweh believe it or not. I just have to live until one or the other happens unless Yahweh gives me rest from the enemies of my Salvation by making them see me the way He sees me in the light of peacemaker and Prophet of Yahweh. I know the Prophet Moses was not activated until he was close to 80 years old, so I've got time to do a work worthy of the spirit of the Prophet. Only God can keep me alive through it.

My enemies are stronger than I am. I was disillusioned to think I was a mighty warrior until I attack my cellmate and ran out of gas ending up on my hands and knees before my cellnate. If the Lord had not told me to trip him he would have won the fight and been alive today. This is not to say anything except that I lost the fight but listened to the Lord who gave me the victory after I had gone as far as I could. Now I feel, even though I won the war I lost. I lost all the chance I had at parole. I lost the chance I had to live in peace without many enemies. I lost my sense of self and security in the system. Was he innocent blood? No, I think not because he was dogging me out, stealing my property sending people to collect money from me for no good reason and thumbing his nose in my face. He was laughing at my religious beliefs. Did he deserve to die that is not for me to decide. All I can say is I felt my hand was forced by God and I was only able to succeed in my task when God spoke to in my ear to him to trip him. I tripped him, he hit his head and I was given a divine advantage over my cellmate. Although I wish he were here today.

Future: What are my plans for the future? To be a prophesying inmate. I am hoping to patch up all my beefs with other inmates by the power of God. I am willing to lay down my life in righteousness not resisting the wicked just like the Bible teaches. I pray for the strength to imitate Jesus and pray forgiveness over those who are killing me as I die. I pray that I can tun the other cheek and submit to the will of God in every

way the Bible teaches us to. This way my behavior will glorify

God in my ending better than in my beginning.

Charity: I was able to get food and canteen in my day. I took

care of the needy and those who wish to borrow I never

refused. I pray that the Lord who saw all these times I gave in

His name, would take those seeds, and make a harvest for me in

the in this world. A harvest of Salvation and holy behavior so

that I can behave in line with the revealed Word of God an

fulfilled my role as a Prophet in Jesus name. I pray that fear and

trouble don't last always and that You would leave me a way to

escape all temptations that come my way so I can show the

Angels that men can overcome by that great Spirit of Yahweh.

Judgment: I do not judge or condemn anyone so I can stand in

the face of my own judgment because God does not judge us

the way we judge each other. Our father has an extreme way of

connecting behavior and behaviors patterns. If you look at

patterns of behavior all sin is connected an equal as disobedience and in a dictatorship, which is what this Kingdom is. Disobedience warrants death to put it out of the Kingdom. So wherever you find yourself on the continent you got it coming. But you can substitute the death of Christ for yourself and circumvent the death you would get. God is good but He is not without wrath. He has an anger that is terrible in his extreme nature, but He is good enough to make ways for his creation to slip past it as He is not prideful. He takes no pride in overcoming anyone and destroying them because He can destroy anyone and all of theirs. There is no mighty one whom the Lord cannot destroy so He is in no rush to repay us for our sins.

The death we earn rather than deserve, because deserve really has nothing to do with it. It is the violations that must be addressed. God has so many people Angels and rulers dependent on His Word that He keeps the letter of it in the Spirit of stability in the heavens. People and Angels need to depend on God so He can provide security for all being. He remains the same as all things revolve around Him. Even the wicked revolve around the Father. The devil presented himself to our Father and ask permission to afflict Job. He also asks permission to trouble us or in our wickedness leave us alone, so we change not and remain in our wickedness unchanged in the ways of righteousness.

Myself. I have troubles more when I'm around the wicket as they make me want to be like them in some ways. I fight to do right but when I am around the wicked, it is less likely for me to do the good I wish to do then when I am alone. So bad company is said to corrupt good morals is sure to corrupt good morals. too true is, no man is an island to himself. For this reason, I perceive the Lord saying seek out isolation by force if necessary and you will not have the pull of the wicked. The call of the wild if you get my meaning. So, I am fixing in my head what ways can I isolation myself and the trip leads back to more violence. However, it is not likely to come to pass as there is nowhere left to go and no place in prison devoid of wickedness. So, I am

stuck. I have been told by spiritual communication violence is

the only way. This I hope is not necessary, I hope. I can stay

clean on my own and not seek out the isolation from people to

isolate from sinners who only respect the sinful.

 I have to remember my cellie and how I wish to bring him back

to the land of the living. I am less certain after I have acted on

the right Spirits word then I was when I am acting on it. I do not

see life on a level playing field. We are at a stark disadvantage

where knowledge meets belief I can believe and think I'm right

and also at the same time be dead wrong. What is it that makes

his belief other than our minds and heart so it is with the mind

we believe an with the mind we make mistakes as well? So,

what can one do except act on his belief and accept the

consequences of his activities on the earth hoping and praying

all the while that the Lord would bless him with insight into his

actions? Wisdom, so to speak, so that one does not stray from

the path his life is supposed to take. Believing in the Power of

YHWH to heal the land and give us control over our minds and help for our weaknesses in our heart but for we all have them and there is no one who has never sinned except Jesus the Christ. So what do I deserve, death? But is up to the Lord to determine what I get in this life and the next. Make no mistake Jesus is coming in His own sweet time and your blood will cry out against you. Will you have any hope with the Son of Man? Will you vow an exalt Him as King of Kings and Lord of Lords? Will you plead His death for your sins? I hope so, as this is the way we win our personal wars in heaven by the Blood of Jesus and our testifying that He died for your sins. Even so, come Lord. We need your You to push back the darkness, expose us to the Light of Your day and help us see what You have hidden and revealed so that seeing they cannot see in hearing they do not hear. So, faith is as fool's gold to the wicked and as hope is every lasting to the righteous, As to all mankind, wisdom is lost except that wisdom which comes from the fear of the Lord with the understanding of keeping Your Commands. Bless Your Name.

Finally: it is my plea that the book of this prophecy is published and read. In hopes that I be quoted as saying Jesus is not weak nor nonviolent. He is coming to rule us with a rod of iron, with discipline and punishment in His Hand He will kill with the Spirit all who do not gather with Him. Yahweh has anger issues to work out on the wicked, He will punish them in the lake of fire. F ear the Lake of fire and affliction forever. Only those who refuse to hear will be gathered for the second death, made for the devil and those who tried to kill off mankind from the very beginning of time. Which is exclusive to the tribulation and travail of planet earth and the people on it. We are the only ones who need time. It is time to repent and follow after the Lord of Glory. There is no other need for time to be measured like a commodity.

 All things are everlasting in nature if it exists now, it always has in some form or fashion existed. Awareness of your existence is all that we lack because the birth and the death of any man is a mystery. Where he goes or where he comes from is mysterious.

All that we know is we came we saw, we live and we will die.

Then we will see the next stage in our humble existence. P raise

Yahweh, submit to His Will as you understand it and you will

live. If you live or lean on your own understanding, you will die.

The mind never stops weighing one thing against another so

there is no cessation of ideas. I stand like a clash of truth with

truth. How can I have faith unless I have understanding> I tell

you unless you take the Word of God like a child takes the word

of a parent you should not see His Glory, The only thing you will

see is contradictions, The minute you look with open eyes and

faith as a child, you will see the connections and dispel the

contradictions overtime. I pray that all would trust God and see

Salvation in this world as we shall all die and face God in his own

time. We will be at His Mercy and we are already at His Mercy

in this world.

 All the deaths, rapes and molestations in this world of the

thieves, and hatred are the manifestations of the wrath of

Yahweh spilling into the world. The punishment of rebellion

known an unknown. We know that some people dwell in ignorance and some live by the light of Yahshua. Those that live in ignorance unknowingly rebel so that their evil is not outright rebellion. Those who do not believe God exists cannot live in conscious rebellion. They walk in darkness though they see and hear, they perceive not and do not take it to heart that which they do. This is not an excuse for we are accountable even if we do not know there is a Law covering our actions. We still are subject to punishment for violating the Law but what about the righteous people> They are not righteous of their own will but of the will of God so that not one person can be righteous by doing good deeds alone because we all have one deed in which we fell short of righteousness, One must be cleansed by the Blood of Jesus. Only then can you claim to be righteous.

 Your claim to be righteous on the account that your wrongs are forgiven. Sin is anything that God says is illegal and in violation of heavens Laws. God's Word is a Law unto itself. it commands obedience by all because He is the Ruler of all. He is not to be questioned or examined because no one is equal to Him. When He has not exalted in Word and indeed Yahshua is equal in authority because He sat down at the right hand of the Father. He is counted for a time as equal to the Father but in Corinthians it is prophesied that the Father, once again will take back His authority and be All in all one again. This is not done because the Great God proud but so He can share in all that He has with His creation and His children so we may not accuse him of being one sided He is honorable and meek in heart although He has all emotions known to man except fear. He knows no fear. He is not able to feel afraid because no one can hurt Him in any way. All that try to do harm to Him, harm themselves. There is no way to cause harm or loss to the Father. Those who try will only gain punishment for trying. Many have tried and many have been condemned for it. I pray that you will hear my voice and fear the Father.

Tremble at His voice He thunders and shakes the earth for any reason He should choose. He is always going to win. Dan never stands in the seat of the defeated. He is forever the Almighty so that only He can do all that He wishes to do and still be considered Righteous. He makes the Law with His Word so He can do no wrong. All who do anything in obedience to Yahweh is in the right not in the wrong. Although they shall be judged by mankind because of their ignorant in knowing what Yahweh told you. It may be that you feel God wants you to violate some law and has instructed you. If God has instructed you, you are bound by the Word of the Lord that came to you. Be very sure you want to risk your all on what you heard because that's exactly what you are doing. If the Father do not come to your aid you are out there on your own as I am out here on my own merit. People choose whether or not to believe me when I say God is speaking to me. My mental illness diagnosis does not help me convince others that I hear God either. I must say that it has dawned on me that although I hear God, I also hear other voices and I have to be careful of what I do, based on the fact that I hear spirits of darkness as well as the Lord.

I cannot explain why I have to be in in the rim of the spiritual

Influences but when God appears then we will not have any

questions and I will no longer act on the voices. I will choose my

behavior by other means than spiritual voices I will lean on the

options of the Holy Spirit and do no more harm. This is the end

of the matter. Treat all people like you wish to be treated.

Amen.

A PRACTICAL

GUIDE TO

REPENTANCE

Romans 13: <u>11</u> And that, knowing the time, that now *it is* high time to awake out of sleep: for now *is* our salvation nearer than when we believed.

<u>12</u> The night is far spent; the day is at hand: let us therefore cast off the

works of darkness and let us put on the

armor of light.

<u>13</u> Let us walk honestly, as in the day,

not in rioting and drunkenness, not in

chambering and wantonness, not in

strife and envying.

<u>14</u> But put ye on the Lord Jesus Christ,

and make not provision for the flesh,

to *fulfil* the lusts *thereof*.

A Practical Guide To Repentance

Table of Content

INTRODUCTION

Dedicated to the Lord God Almighty for His righteousness, insomuch as the devil that tricked Eve into breaking the kingdom rule. Breaking the only kingdom rule should cause one to forever suffer in the end and in the present suffer the fruitless repeating of his actions without hope of putting away from the kingdom those who were more precious than he.

Men, the only ones more precious than he before the Lord. And while the Father was not able to come close to those who did not obey the kingdom rule, His son has come close that through

Him we may understand the rule of the kingdom.

That nothing in existence shall stand before the

Lord, lest it perishes before him! [Romans 14:11-23]

WHAT IS REPENTANCE?

Repentance is the act of turning away from something due to self-reproach or the reproach of another. The American Heritage Dictionary says to feel regret or self-reproach for what one has done, also to change for the better result of remorse or contrition for one's sins. The Lord has condemned the world because of sin. He sent His word so that you could understand what it is He does not want you to do and commanded that you repent of your sins! Revelations 9:20-21 says: "And the rest of the men who were killed by these plagues, neither repented of the works of their hands, that is to say, the worship of devils and idols of gold and silver and brass and stone and of wood, which can neither see nor hear, nor repented of their murders nor of their witchcraft nor of their fornication nor of their thefts."

There is no way to misunderstand what this said if you go back and read the definition of the word repent. John 3:16: "For God so loved the world that He gave His only begotten son, so that whoever believes in Him should not perish but have eternal life". And I say this is true; you must believe Him! If you are to do what He said for you to do. John 3:35-36: "The Father loves the Son and has placed everything into His hand. He who believes in the son has eternal life; and he who does not obey the Son shall not see life, but the wrath of God shall remain on him". Now in John 3:16, the Lord said whoever believes has eternal life and He said the same in John 3:36: He who does not obey the son shall not see life. If you believe Him, you must obey. The TWO CANNOT be separated at all. Jesus is Lord!

Finally, the Lord said to you, "How do you say He is your Lord and you do not do what He says?" Luke 6:46: "Why do you call me My Lord, My Lord and do not do what I say?"

II

WHAT IS FAITH IN JESUS?

John 14:21-24: "He who has my commandments with him and obeys them is the one who loves me; he who loves me will be loved by my father, and I will love him and reveal myself to him." Judas (not Iscariot) said to him, "My Lord, why is it that you will reveal yourself to us and not to the world?" Jesus answered, saying to him, "He who loves me keeps my word; and my Father will love him, and we will come to him and make a place of abode with him. But he who does not love me does not keep my Word and this Word which you hear is not My own but the Fathers who sent me."

Faith in Jesus is believing what He said would happen to those who obeyed Him will happen to them. Also, what He said would happen to those who did not believe what He said would happen to them. This IS the faith of the Lord Jesus: LIFE to those who repent and death to those who do not believe His word.

The American Heritage Dictionary says: Faith: a confident belief or trust in a person, idea, or thing. Also, loyalty, allegiance as well as often secure belief in God and acceptance of God's will and a religion.

Now the Bible says, in Hebrews Chapter 11:1: Now faith is the substance of things hoped for, as it was the substance of things which have come to pass and it is the evidence of things not seen.

Now faith is the substance of things hoped for… Before we go on, let's see what the American Heritage Dictionary says substance means. Substance: a. That which has mass and occupies space matter. b. A material of a particular kind or constitution. 2. The essence; gist. 3. That which is solid and practical. 4. Density; body. 5. Material possessions; wealth.

With substance defined, we now can go back to what the Spirit said in Hebrews 11:1: Faith is the substance of things hoped for. Does the Christian believe in Jesus and hope for the eternal life he promised those who obey him? Yes, THAT IS YOUR FAITH. It is easily defined as believing that if you obey Jesus, you will become a son to the Lord.

But BEWARE lest any mislead you! Hebrews 11:6: Without faith, man cannot please God; for he who comes to God must believe that He is and that He is a rewarder of those who seek Him.

Now if you have faith in Jesus, you will please God! Because you believe that if you do not repent because of His Word you will be tortured with flame and fear day and night forever.

Revelation 14:11: And the smoke of their torment will rise forever and ever; and those who worship the beast and his image will have no rest day or night. Faith in the Lord says that will happen, period. If you do not believe this why would you obey Jesus Christ?

Revelation 22:16: I, Jesus, have sent My angel to testify to you these things in the churches. I am the root and the offspring of David, the bright and morning star.

Jesus said in Matthew 21:21: Truly I say to you if you have faith

and do not doubt, etc. ..

Faith is the substance of hope in Jesus' word; obey Him and do

not doubt.

James 1:25: But whoever looks into the perfect law of liberty

and abides in it is not merely a hearer of the Word which can be

forgotten but a doer of the work and this man shall be blessed

in his labor.

The Lord's faith is the teachings of Jesus Christ!

III

WHAT IS THE HOLY SPIRIT?

"Let my cry come before Thee, O Lord; save me according to Thy Word. Let my supplication come before Thee; deliver me according to Thy word. My tongue shall speak of Thy Word; for all Thy commandments are righteous. My lips shall speak of Thy praise when Thou has taught me Thy commandments. Let Thine hand help me for I have delighted in Thy statutes. I have longed for Thy salvation, O Lord; and I meditate on Thy law. Let my soul live and it shall praise Thee and let Thy judgments help me. I have gone astray like a lost sheep; seek Thy servant for I do not forget Thy commandments." Ps. 119:169-176.

The Holy Spirit is the Lord omnipresent. The American Heritage Dictionary says this: Omnipresent: present everywhere.

Mark 9:37: Whoever receives a child like this in my name, He receives me; and He who receives me does not receive me, but Him who Has sent me.

Jesus claimed to be one with God the Father and that He was the Father and this is true. The HOLY SPIRIT is the Father; our Father, the very Spirit that gives all life the very Lord God is the Spirit.

Revelation 22:6: And he said to me, these sayings are faithful and true and the Lord God who is the Spirit of the prophets sent His angel to show to His servants the things which shortly must come to pass.

John 4:24: For God is a spirit and those who worship Him must worship Him in Spirit and in Truth. That is how the Father can have a relationship with all His children. If a man receives the Spirit of the Lord, He is one with that Spirit. The same spirit that Jesus called Father is the Spirit that comes to those who obey the words of Jesus Christ. The power of the Lord is the Spirit of the Lord!

Acts 1:2 Until the day when He ascended, after He, through the Holy Spirit had given commandments to the Apostles whom He had chosen.

The American Heritage Dictionary says: through 1. In one side and out another side of. 2. In the midst of. 3. By way of. 4. By means of agency of. 5. Here and therein, around. 6. From the beginning to the end of. 7. Done or finished with.

As an adverb- through: From one end or side to another end or side. 2. From the beginning to end. 3. Through the whole extent or thickness. 4. To a conclusion.

Jesus plainly said He did nothing of His own will but that He always did the will of His father because He and His Father were one. John 20:17: Jesus said to her, do not come near me for I have not yet ascended to my Father, but go to my brethren and say to them, I am ascending to my Father and your Father and my God and your God. Here He said His father and your Father, His God, and your God. Is this a contradiction? No, but you must listen.

Acts 1:2: After He through the Holy Spirit had given commandments. What is the Holy Spirit? Revelations 22:6: And the Lord God (who is the Spirit) of the prophets sent...

The Lord Jesus said in John 20:17: But go to my brethren and say to them, I am ascending to my Father and your Father and my God and your God. And we see that He gave His commands (through the Spirit) and He told His followers in Acts 1:8: But when the (Holy Spirit) comes upon you, you shall receive power and you shall be witnesses to me, etc. What then! Then you too shall be the Lord's children. My father and your father!

John 3:6: What is born of the flesh is flesh and what is born of spirit is spirit. So, if you receive the Spirit, you are no longer flesh but spirit. So as the Lord Jesus was one with the Spirit or one with the Father, so you shall be one with the Father just like He said!

Matthew 11:40: Whoever receives you, receives me and whoever receives me, receives Him who sent me.

Matthew 25:45: Truly I say to you, insomuch as you did not do it to one of these least ones, you also did not do it to me. This all points to the Spirit becoming one with people who believe what Jesus said. And in John 6:45: We are told again, "For it is written in the prophet, they shall all be taught by God. Everyone therefore who hears from the Father and learns from Him will come to me."

The Lord Jesus and the Father are one by the Spirit. You can only become one with Jesus by the Father; by the same Spirit and then you too will always do the will of the Father as Jesus always does the will of the Father. 1 Corinthians 12:7: But the manifestation of the Spirit is given to every man to help him. Verse 12 of the same chapter says: For as the Body is one and has many members and all the members of the body, even though many, are one Body, so also is Christ. All those who receive the Spirit are one with the Spirit… one with the Lord. 1 John 3:24: The Spirit says whoever keeps His commandments will be guarded by Him and will dwell in Him. And by this, we know that He abides in us by the Spirit, which He has given us.

Now let's check one point, Jesus said He always did, the will of another, His father without fail, how could that be?

1 John 4:9: Whoever is born of God does not commit sin because God's seed is in him and he cannot sin because he is born of God.

I quote: "Truly I say unless you are born of water and spirit, you cannot enter into the Kingdom of God, of your father and my father, your God and my God."

Who can receive the Spirit? Well, here is what Jesus said in Matthew 5:38: You have heard it is said, an eye for an eye, and a tooth for a tooth. But I say to you that you should not resist evil; but whoever strikes you on the cheek, turn the other also. 40. And if anyone wishes to sue you at the court and take away your shirt, let him have your robe also. 41. Whoever compels you to carry a burden for a mile, go with him two. 42. Whoever asks from you, give him and whoever wishes to borrow from you, do not refuse him. 43. You have heard that it is said, be kind to your friend and hate your enemy. 44. But I say to you, love your enemies, bless anyone who curses you, do good to anyone who hates you, and pray for those who carry you away by force and persecute you. Why did he say to do this? He said plainly in the next verse: 45. So that you may become sons of your Father which is in heaven...Do you believe in what the Spirit says to you?

Beware lest anyone mislead you. If you believe Jesus told you how to become sons of God, just do it!

IV

WHAT IS THE LOVE OF GOD?

Matthew 6:14: For if you forgive men their faults, your Father in heaven will also forgive you. But if you do not forgive men, neither will your Father forgive even your faults.

John 17:20-21: I am not making requests for these alone, but also for the sake of those who believe in me through their word. So that they all may be one; Just as thou, my Father (art with me) and I am (with Thee) that they also may be one with us.

The love of God is to do what He asks of us. That is the love of God. In James 1:12, the Spirit says: Blessed is the man who endures temptations; for when he is tested, he shall receive the crown of life which God has promised to those who love him.

But that does not say anything about love. Well, let's see what the American Heritage Dictionary says. Love: 1. Deep affection and warm feelings for another. 2. The emotion of sex and romance; strong sexual desire for another person. 3. A beloved person. 4. A strong fondness or enthusiasm. 5. Sports: a zero score in tennis. Verb: loved, loving. 1. To feel love (for). 2. To like or desire enthusiastically. Idiom: In love, feeling love, enamored, lovable. Adj.: loveless.

But that says nothing of doing what someone else wants. How can I say that to love God you must obey the Lord Jesus Christ! Why should you believe in me!

You only need to believe Jesus, in order to be saved! O.K. I said that myself! Jesus said in John 15:8: In this the Father will be glorified that you bear abundant fruit and be my disciples. 9. Just as my Father has loved Me; I also have loved you. Abide in my love. 10. If you keep my commandment, you will abide in my love, even as I have kept my Father's commandments and abide in His love.

Do you believe Jesus Christ! This is what He said, the love of God was, God sent His son; so all who believed in Him would not perish! Do you believe what Jesus says? If you do, you will believe Him when He says; that you do not love Him if you do not keep His commands. In John 16:14 he says: You are my friends if you do everything, I command you.

Well that does not leave much room to the devil or the blind guides to lie on Jesus in His Name does it? But let's hear Him one more time in John 14:14-17, He tells you how to get the Spirit of God for yourself: If you ask me in My own Name, I will do it. If you love me, keep my commandments and I will ask of my father and He will give you another comforter to be with you forever, even the Spirit of truth, whom the world cannot receive because it has not seen Him and does not know Him, but you know Him because He abides with you and is in you.

Now, if you believe Jesus was not a liar, will you keep His commands?

O.K. Alright. I still have not shown that Jesus said that you did not love Him if you did not obey Him. I am sorry. Do you not trust me? Have I lied at all so far? Ok, Ok... The Lord said trust no man, well believe that because many will lie in His Name and modify the Words of Jesus!

John 14:23: Jesus answered, saying to Him, He who loves me keeps my Word; and my Father will love him, and we will come to him and make a place of abode with him. But he who does not love me, does not keep my Word; and this Word which you hear is not my own but the Father who sent me.

Well how could the very words He spoke not be His own? Again, He spoke plainly in John 16:32: For behold, the hour is coming and it has now come, when you will be dispersed, every man to his own country, and you will leave me alone and yet I am never alone because the Father is with me.

Well, do you believe what Jesus said that if you ask Him and keep His commands, He will ask for you to be one with the Father as He is.

Who is Jesus Christ to command anyone? Is He Lord or what? He says His Father sent Him so how is He Lord? Well, in Luke 22:69: From henceforth the Son of man will sit at the right hand of the Power of God. Well! What is the right hand of someone's

power? In Matthew 23:44 we read: The Lord said to my Lord, sit

thou at my right hand until I put your enemies under Your feet.

That does not tell us what the right hand is does it? David said

of the Lord in Psalms 16:8: I have set the Lord always before me

because he is at my right hand, I shall not be moved. And in

verse 11: Thou wilt show me the path of life and I shall be filled

with the joy of thy countenance with the pleasure of victory of

Thy right hand.

THERE GOES THAT HAND AGAIN.

The right hand is the authority or power of someone. Luke

11:28: He said to her, blessed are they who hear the Word of

God and keep it!

V

WHAT IS THE FEAR OF THE LORD?

Exodus 15:3: The Lord is a mighty warrior. The Lord is His

Name.

Genesis 7:23-24: And every living thing was destroyed that was

upon the face of the ground, both man and animals and the

creeping things and the fowl of the air; they were destroyed

from the earth; and Noah only remained, and those who were

with him in the ark. And the waters prevailed upon the earth a

hundred and fifty days.

Luke 19:27: But those my enemies, who were not willing that I

should rule over them bring here and kill them before me.

Romans 15:11 For it is written, as I live said the Lord, every knee

shall bow to me and every tongue shall confess to me.

What is the fear of the Lord? Let us first see what the American

Heritage Dictionary says: Fear 1a. A feeling of agitation and

anxiety caused by the presence of imminence of danger. B. A

state marked by this feeling. 2. A feeling of disquiet or apprehension. 3. Reverence or piety towards a deity. 4. A reason for dread or apprehension. Verb. 1. To be afraid of. 2. To be apprehensive about. 3. To be in awe of 4. To expect: I fear you are wrong.

Is this what God wants you to feel of Him? Can anyone tell you that a loving God sent His son to die for you and that He still plans on punishing those who do not fear Him and what He says? Would He actually torment people forever? I will not answer this straight out until we have looked at His track record as it is written. In the end, you may be able to tell me before I answer the question for you. Let us take in account some of the Lord's actions.

In Leviticus chapter 10, Aaron's two sons offered incense to the Lord. They were Levites, the priestly family. They simply offer this incense at the wrong time; and not how He said to do it. What happened? He burned them to death. Now, Moses, knowing God, told Aaron not to shave his head or tear his clothes or wrath might come upon all the people. So, neither

Aaron or his two remaining sons mourned their loved ones. And

he also said they should stay in the Lord's tabernacle or God

might kill them too! They did not test it! They stayed in the

Lord's house.

Well, let's go further in Numbers 1:4. The Lord's people were

afraid to fight and kill the people who owned the promised

land. They were former slaves, not warriors, so they said let's go

back and subject ourselves to the Egyptians. So He made them

walk around the borders of it until they all died. All of the ones

who were old enough to fight except the two who wanted to

fight. Only those that did not fear survived the march!

In Numbers 16, there was a man, Korah was his name, he felt

that since God has chosen all of Israel to be holy that Moses

should not exalt himself. So, he challenged the position God

gave Moses. So when they got together to see what the Lord

would do, the Lord said for Moses to step away from the people

so He could kill all of them and start over with just Moses and

Aaron. But Moses, as you will see often, begged the Lord not to kill them all for Korah's actions. The Lord agreed not to kill them all but said to stay away from Korah and two other's houses and to warn the people to do the same. The Lord caused the ground to swallow all three households. Yes, all three households. Then their wives and kids along with all they had!

Let's go on further in the Word. There were 250 men that offered incense to the Lord that were swallowed up and buried. They burned incense to the Lord. The Lord responded by burning them in the pit. The rest of the people blamed Moses and the Lord killed 14,700 more in answer to the anger of those who were mad because of Korah and his followers. Wait! Weren't these the same ones forced already to circle those fearsome people they did not want to attack? Yes! Let us move on:

In Numbers 21, the people complained again because the bread God fed them was not good enough. The Lord sent snakes to bite them so they would die. Moses again went to the Lord for the people so they would not all die. The Lord made a way. Let's go further into the scriptures to see what else is written a few years later. But first let me give you one part of Moses' farewell address.

Duet 7:21: "You shall not be afraid of them, for the Lord your God is among you a great and terrible God." Looks like something is wrong with the loving God! Let us move on.

In Joshua 6, the Lord had the people take over Jericho and destroy it. But how did He say to do it and what did they destroy? Verse 21: "And they utterly destroyed all that were in the city, both men and women, young and old and oxen and sheep and asses with the edge of the sword. Saving only the woman's family who saved two of the Jews in return for her family's lives.

Stay with me, we have a little way to go yet! But let's try skipping a few generations or so!

In 2 Kings 2, there were little boys, a lot of them making fun of Elisha, the prophet. He cursed them in the name of the Lord and two bears came out of the woods and killed 42 of them.

Ok, I'm not going to go and recount every time God killed people for things like this or worse or whatever reasons He found to be reason to kill many or few. But let's find maybe one more. Alright?

In 1 Kings 21, the Lord told the prophet Elijah to say the King Ahab, "I will pluck one by one your children. Every male child and the dogs shall eat Jezebel, your wife, in the inheritance of Jezreel. All of those who belong to you that die in the city, the dogs will eat! And those that die in the field, the birds will eat! And He did it!

Well, it's time for me to tell you if He wants you to fear him. Yes, He does! For your own good. Why else would He record all these things for you to read. So, you will know how to act if He should command you. Because those who do not regard him as one to be feared cannot depend on Him for protection and safety. Who can depend on a weak and passive Lord to ever hold safe a kingdom for anyone forever!

One last look at the Lord. He commanded death for many sins in the Law! What types of things were given death sentences? Deut. 17:2-5 tells you those who worship things like the sun, moon, or anything in heaven which he has not commanded are to be stoned to death. They had to assemble together and stone them to death. Why? They did not fear Him!

In Deut. 21:18-21, the Lord tells the people what to do with their stubborn or rebellious children. What was it he commanded? That the father and mother bring Him to an assembly. And all the men shall stone him. Ok, once more I will pick out a law and punishment, the Lord commanded!

Leviticus 20:14: "And if a man takes a wife and her mother, it is wickedness. They shall be burned with fire. Both he and they, that there may be no wickedness among you.

There is one thing that connects the people here in this chapter. They did not fear the Lord. Shouldn't you reverence the Lord instead of fearing Him? Let Him answer for Himself?

Deut. 19:20-21: And those who remain shall hear and fear and shall never again commit any such an evil thing among you. And your eye shall not pity; but life shall be for life, eye for eye, tooth for tooth, hand for hand, foot for foot.

But we see that when Jesus gave His life, all punishment was put on hold so that all should have a chance to repent and come to the Lord through Jesus, being that the Father inside of the Son by His Spirit together paid for our sins and by the stripes Jesus suffered we are healed!

But those my enemies who were not willing that I should rule over them bring here and kill before me! Luke 19:27

VI

WHAT IS THE SPIRIT OF ADOPTION?

In whom, you also have heard the Word of truth, which is the gospel for your salvation; in Him you have believed, so you are sealed with the Holy Spirit that was promised, which is the pledge of our inheritance for the salvation of those who are saved and for the glory of His honor. (Eph. 1:13-14)

American Heritage Dictionary: Pledge: 1. A formal promise. 2. Something considered as security to guarantee payment of a debt or obligation. 3. One who has been accepted for membership in a club, fraternity, or sorority, etc.

And He marked his disciples (us) with His love to be His from the beginning and adopted us to be sons through Jesus Christ as it pleased His will (Eph. 1:5)

The Spirit of adoption is the same as the Holy Spirit, also the anointing is that very same Spirit. That is why you must be born of the Spirit. Jesus taught in John 4:24: For God is Spirit; and those who worship Him must worship Him in spirit and in truth.

Let us go to the dictionary for worship. American Heritage Dictionary: Worship 1a. Reverent love and devotion for a deity or sacred object. B. The ceremonies of prayers by which this love is expressed. 2. Ardent devotion; adoration, his worship of fame…etc.

That said, the Spirit of adoption is the pledge (see definition at chapter beginning) of the Holy Spirit that comes into you to teach you everything you need to know and to let you know that you are the son of God born of His Spirit and this is the power of the children of God. This is why the Lord said to those who wish to become children of God and enter into His kingdom must do so as a child. If the Holy Spirit is to live in His children, He must be the Father and you must be the child.

Luke 18:17: "Truly I say to you, he who will not receive the kingdom of God like a little child will never enter into it."

And when the Spirit comes upon you as your seal, you will begin to communicate with your father. He is one with all of His children. In John 16:23, the Lord says, "On that day, you will not ask me anything. Truly, truly, I say to you that whatever you ask my Father in my Name, He will give it to you."

The very Spirit of the Lord will be with those who believe that these things are true. Now if the Lord is to live in you and be your Father, you must be willing to be the child and accept His discipline. The Lord will not allow His children to lead Him, you must be led by Him. He is the Almighty God, and He will not live with the person who is not willing to give Him their right hand and become obedient to Him. He cannot serve you and be your Father as well!

2 Cor. 6:16-18: What harmony has the Temple of God with idols? For you are the Temple of the living God; as it is said, I will dwell in them and walk in them and I will be their God and they shall be My people. Wherefore come out from among them and be separate, says the Lord and touch not the unclean thing and I

will receive you and will be a Father to you and you shall be My sons and daughters said the Lord Almighty.

This is why He can say: He disciplines all His children. Because the very Spirit that is given as a pledge to His children is the Holy Spirit says to Him, teach me Father in Jesus' Name. Show me what to do with you Father in Jesus' Name. Why can you ask of the Father of creation, the God of all flesh, and receive what you ask?

1 John 3:22: and whatever we ask, we receive from him because we keep His commandments and do those things that are pleasing to him.

So, are you just supposed to receive the Spirit and then move on your own way? Not according to the Bible; that cannot be. He is supposed to teach you all things so much so that you will not need a teacher. The anointing will teach you all things. How can I be sure? Well, in John 2:27, the Spirit says "And you also, (if) the anointing which you have received from Him abides among you, you need no one to teach you; that same anointing which is of God will teach you all things; it is the Truth and there is no lie in it and even as I have taught you, abide in it." For I was hungry and you did not give me food; I was thirsty and you did not give me drink; I was a stranger and you did not clothe me; I was sick and in prison and you did not visit me. Matt. 42:44

Matt. 24:45, "Then he will answer and say to them, truly I say to you, Inasmuch as you did not do it to one of these least ones you also did not do it to me."

John 15:10, "If you keep my commandments, you will abide in my love, even as I have kept my Father's commandments and abide in his love."

WAIT! LOOK! But those, my enemies, who were not willing that I should rule over them bring here and kill them before me. Luke 19:27

***********************AMEN! *****************

VII

A PRACTICAL WAY TO STUDY WHAT JESUS TAUGHT

When starting to study the Bible, you can't go wrong with the Words of Jesus. He is the one who you must believe in! So learn first what all He said before you decide whether or not you want anything to do with what He says! You cannot believe me if you do not know what I said!!

Next, when you really want to know what you read, a dictionary is the best way to be sure you know what was said. The words are in there! For most Bibles, please use one for your own good!

Matthew 5:32, 34, 39-45,48. 6:3; 6:17,32. 7:1-2, 17; 9:13; 15:10, 17-19, 19:9, 18. 21:21-22, 23:8, 24:26

Mark 4:24; 7:20-23, 8:38, 10:11, 29-30, 11:25; 13:5; 11:21-23.

Luke 6:27-38, 46; 12:4-5; 13:3; 14:26-27, 16: 18; 17:3-4, 23; 19:27

John 4:24; 6:29, 10:18, 34-35, 12:25; 16:23, 27, 32.

Luke 19:27: But those my enemies who were not willing that I should rule over them, bring here, and kill them before me.

The Father cannot be tempted by what He does not like. If He comes to you, remember He can control all things within you by power. He is Almighty God, not by any other means. He is Almighty. Ask Him to not let you want what He does not like. He will do it for you!

TIME FOR A FABLE!

The Almighty God, being a Spirit, was searching throughout His creation, when He came to the rain forest where He hid himself within a special bird and began to see and feel all that the bird saw and felt. The bird was not aware that he was Almighty. So, when the tiger came by, he began to tremble. And the Almighty became agitated because of the tiger's reasoning to cause the bird to fear before he ate him. So, the Almighty God caused the tiger to feel a great fear and he ran away! The bird, unaware of the Almighty, began to feel pride and chased the tiger and cornered him. This displeased the Almighty, so he removed the fear he placed on the tiger. The tiger being hungry, immediately ate the bird and swallowed him whole. The Almighty began to console the tiger for his nerves were shaken Almighty bird.

Blessings From the Editor

When The book, A PRACTICAL GUIDE TO REPENTANCE by Meeko Carraway, was presented to the Elders and others, there was no reply many. Some perhaps were stunned at the ending verse. The Messiah is quoted saying: "But those mine enemies, which would not that I should reign over them, bring hither, and slay *them* before me." Is this the message that has and still does influence many to burn crosses, go on witch hunts, start riots to kill rioters, or otherwise persecute those whom "they" determine are not believers? Let us look at some other verses before we decide. The Church is denoted as the Bride of the Messiah. She is then depicted as feminine with the Messiah as the Husbandman, Protector, Leader, and Head of the whole Body or Assembly. May we all, bring mankind to the Messiah in prayer always.

Revelations 12: _5_ And she brought forth a man child, who was to rule all nations with a rod of iron: and her child was caught up unto God, and *to* his throne. _6_ And the woman fled into the wilderness, where she hath a place prepared of God, that they should feed her there a thousand two hundred *and* threescore days.

We might note that this is Satan after the believers in the Messiah. The woman represents the Church, Saints, followers of the Messiah. Who can determine who will come to believe? Some are babes in Christ. Others are unbelievers without hope of repentance and redemption. Only the Father can make this determination. He only can judge hearts. Let us look at another woman that may help many who are judgmental to come to repentance, be still and wait patiently for the Messiah to harvest the souls of the true repentant believers, in these last days, prior to final judgment.

John 8: _3_ And the scribes and Pharisees brought unto him a woman taken in adultery; and when they had set her in the midst, _4_ They say unto him, Master, this woman was taken in

adultery, in the very act. _5_ Now Moses in the law commanded

us, that such should be stoned: but what sayest thou? _6_This

they said, tempting him, that they might have to accuse him.

But Jesus stooped down, and with *his* finger wrote on the

ground, *as though he heard them not._7_* So when they

continued asking him, he lifted up himself, and said unto them,

He that is without sin among you, let him first cast a stone at

her. _8_And again he stooped down and wrote on the ground. _9_

And they which heard *it*, being convicted by *their*

own conscience, went out one by one, beginning at the

eldest, *even* unto the last: and Jesus was left alone, and the

woman standing in the midst. _10_ When Jesus had lifted up

himself, and saw none but the woman, he said unto her,

Woman, where are those thine accusers? hath no man

condemned thee? _11_ She said, No man, Lord. And Jesus said

unto her, neither do I condemn thee: go, and sin no more.

Let us all come to repentance, **go and sin no more**, least we be numbered and condemned among the sinners who were not able to cast the first stone.

Galatians 1: 1Paul, an apostle, (not of men, neither by man, but by Jesus Christ, and God the Father, who raised him from the dead;) 2And all the brethren which are with me, unto the churches of Galatia:

3Grace *be* to you and peace from God the Father, and *from* our Lord Jesus Christ, 4Who gave himself for our sins, that he might deliver us from this present evil world, according to the will of God and our Father: 5To whom *be* glory for ever and ever. Amen.

No Other Gospel

6 I marvel that ye are so soon removed from him that called you into the grace of Christ unto another gospel: 7 Which is not another; but there be some that trouble you, and would pervert the gospel of Christ. 8 But though we, or an angel from heaven, preach any other gospel unto you than that which we have

preached unto you, let him be accursed. **9** As we said before, so say I now again, If any *man* preach any other gospel unto you than that ye have received, let him be accursed.

10 For do I now persuade men, or God? or do I seek to please men? for if I yet pleased men, I should not be the servant of Christ.

Editor: Doctor Shirley Moore

Blessings to the Author and Prophet Meeko Carraway and the readers of this book.